Corvette

FROM BLUE FLAME SIX TO ZR1

By Bonsall & Zavitz

GALLERY BOOKS
An Imprint of W. H. Smith Publishers Inc.
112 Madison Avenue
New York City 10016

CONTENTS

© Copyright 1988 in U.S.A. by Bookman Dan!, Inc.
Published in the United States of America by Bookman Publishing, an
Imprint of Bookman Dan Inc.
P. O. Box 13492, Baltimore, MD 21203

Exclusive Distribution by Gallery Books,
an Imprint of W. H. Smith Publishers Inc.
112 Madison Avenue, New York City, NY 10016

ISBN 0-8317-1793-9

Printed in the United States of America

PREFACE

Corvette, the car created 35 years ago as a launch platform for its engines, is off on another escapade and 'Vette-ophiles the world over have been talking about little else for months. A Chevy V-8 with dual overhead camshafts. All aluminum. Thirty-two valves. Docile at idle. A demon under power. So strong they redid the rear end to accommodate more rubber. Code-named LT5. Nicknamed the "King of the Hill." A legend before its time. The 1989 Corvette ZR1.

Ed Cole would approve.

A new Corvette is always an exciting event, and especially so for this newest 'Vette powerplant, because of its anticipated performance levels.

After all, this will be the first time the Corvette has ever been offered as two different models. Something special must be on the way, perhaps even as special as the reception of the original Corvette at its first public appearance in the 1953 Detroit Motorama. Designated EX-122, Chevy PR man Myron Scott named it the Corvette.

The first 'Vette engine was a warmed-over production 3.8 liter in-line six, right out of the production sedans. Three sidedraft Carter carburetors bumped the power up to 150 hp and it was mated to the 2-speed Powerglide automatic. Performance wasn't much to write home about--the quarter mile came in 17.9 sec at 77 mph. Top speed was listed at 108 mph.

In 1955, the legendary 195 hp, 265 cid V-8 appeared as an option. With a single two-barrel carburetor, the quarter mile times dropped to 16.7 sec at 83 mph and top speed increased to 118 mph.

Specifications alone cannot begin to describe the 265 V-8. It formed the basis for generations of racing engines and was soon to be found in every form of competition. Its short stroke allowed unheard-of revs and it quickly became the foundation on which countless hot rod parts businesses were built.

In 1957, the first Rochester fuel injection showed up on the 283 cid version of this engine. By the end of the 1950s, power from the 283 had crept up to 290 hp and sales responded by breaking through the 10,000 unit barrier.

Early in the 1960s, Corvette engines topped the 300 hp mark, with a fuel-injected, 11.1:1 compression 283 rated at a whopping 315 hp. There was more to come.

In 1962, the engine displacement increased to 327 cid, with 360 optional horsepower available. This trend continued on through the 1965 Sting Ray , which offered 425 hp from 396 cid (the only year the 396 was offered), then moved on into the era of the 427 big block.

The big block options culminated in the awesome L-88. This killer engine had aluminum heads and manifold, 850 cfm Holley center pivot float carb, 12.5:1 compression. It reached its zenith in the 1969 Stingray ZL-1 option where it was rated at 430 hp.

Early in the 1970s, emissions control became the dictating factor in all Detroit engine design. Even though displacement increased to 454 cid in 1970, power was down to 390 hp. In 1972, the same 454 engine was rated at 270 hp due to the new smog controls.

By the late 1970s and early 1980s, the 'Vette engine was standardized at 350 cid and the 220 hp L-82 was capable of 0-60 mph in the mid-sixes.

These trends are indicative of the change in engine philosophies for Corvette during the past two decades. Fuel was cheap and plentiful in the '60s. Sales seemed directly linked to power and this, in turn, gave designers free reign to produce wonderful fantasies such as the L-88.

Everything changed dramatically in the early 1970s. Engine size and power plummeted as fuel efficiency became the operative term.

The 350 "small block" in the current-generation 'Vette is again beginning to approach some of the performance figures of the '60s, but it's doing so in a much different way. It delivers power fuel-efficiently and with controlled emissions.

Much of the credit for these accomplishments rests with electronic engine controls, which

Below, the very first engineering sketch of what was to become the Corvette. A few months earlier, Chevy engineers had begun to research fiberglass and actually built a 1952 Chevy convertible entirely of that material. Their success made the Corvette project possible.

allow engineers to closely regulate the combustion mixture with closed loop controls. New age manual transmissions with additional gears have also been used to optimize performance and economy.

Corvette engineers also recognize the limitations of the existing small block V-8 in terms of newer "world technologies." To capture this technology, outside firms were contacted with requests to bring a quantum-leap in engine to Chevrolet.

No power levels were specified at this point. Corvette engineers were comfortable with the performance of the current car. They wanted significant increases, but power was the last parameter considered. The thrust was the need to expand the envelope--to push technological boundaries far beyond what was expected of a production car.

The result of these requests is the 1989 LT5 engine. The genesis

dates to a meeting in the spring of '85 between Tony Rudd of lotus and the Corvette Group, ostensibly to discuss Lotus 4-valve heads for the small block engine.

After lengthy study, Mr. Rudd counterproposed a "fresh-sheet-of-paper" engine--one that would meet Chevrolet targets for power without getting entangled in gas-guzzler considerations.

Four main objectives were set for the LT5 engine program:

• Create a car that is second to none in acceleration--nothing less than the fastest production car in the world.

• Achieve that performance without sacrificing driveability--not only at the high end, where you expect fast cars to do well, but at the low end, too.

• Package this leading-edge performance and driveability into an engine that could still deliver great fuel economy.

• And, finally, design this engine to fit between the rails of the existing Corvette's engine compartment--a brand-new engine, but not one that would require a totally new car.

This book tells how that goal was met within the context of the 35-year history of the Corvette, America's greatest sportscar. It is an exciting story--and not just because the cars themselves are so intrinsically exciting, although a brief glance through the pages of this book will amply prove that. The authors hope you will derive as much enjoyment from reading this book as they did from putting it all together. Enjoy!

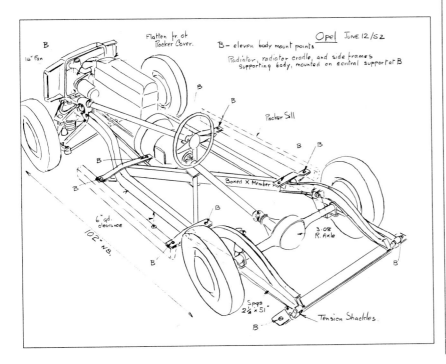

Chapter One

THE FIRST OF THE BREED

Unlike some years in the American auto industry, 1953 brought with it several new models. There was a bit of a prestige war going on at this time and sporty models were the fad of the moment. The results of this were several, but most notably the Cadillac Eldorado, the Oldsmobile Fiesta, the Buick Skylark, the Packard Caribbean--and, of course, the Chevrolet Corvette.

The Oldsmobile Fiesta hardly lasted the year and Buick's Skylark flew off into oblivion within two years, although the name was destined to make numerous curtain calls on different products. The Packard Caribbean hung in there for a while, but disappeared when the real Packards slid into history in

Left, the four cars shown at the GM Motorama. From the top: Corvettes with and without detachable hardtops, the Nomad wagon and the Corvair fastback.

Right, one of the earliest Corvette magazine ads dating from October, 1954.

Following pages, Chevy publicists loved shots showing masses of Corvettes, like these 1954 models photographed in Detroit. Note the Chevy billboard in the distance.

1956. The Cadillac Eldorado has survived, but only after trying various segments of the market with different types of cars. The Chevrolet Corvette, alone among this group, has remained in continuous production since 1953 without deviating from its original concept. That is no mean achievement but, then, the Corvette is no mean car.

The Corvette got off to a

Above, an early Corvette
publicity shot showing the full
array of colors available in 1953:
Polo White.

Right, the Blue Flame Six engine. Note the three carbs.

rather shaky start, though. First of all, the name itself was a bit improbable. It is ancient history now, but the Corvette was named after a type of warship, albeit a fast one, and that seemed odd at the time. Another, more substantial, problem was the construction material used. The Corvette, as everyone knows, had a fiberglass body at a time when the public was hardly used to such material for children's pedal cars, let alone real cars. Thus, the Corvette flew brashly in the face of public prejudice in favor of good old fashioned sheetmetal.

The Corvette was also a sportscar, a genre considered fairly eccentric in that conformist era and a type no major American automaker had ever built before, especially a mainstream automaker such as Chevrolet.

Certain European manufacturers had successfully marketed sportscars in the United States in the early postwar period--

most notably MG and Jaguar--but the big American manufacturers had demonstrated no interest or talent. The typical Detroit car of the period was about as far removed from a sportscar as one could get and the Chevrolet was as close to being the typical American car as any car in 1953. So, the announcement of the Corvette was met with general skepticism, to say the least. Sportscar afficianados doubted Chevrolet even knew how to make a true sportscar.

In particular, sportscar afficianados sneered at Chevy's "stovebolt" six engine, a powerplant that had been around since 1929 and was rugged, smooth and reasonably economical, but hardly noted for performance. Furthermore, the addition of Powerglide automatic transmission as standard equipment was sacrilege of the highest order. Sportscars were supposed to have

11

Left, another mass phalanx of Corvettes tying up traffic in Detroit. Also rumored to be a still from the B-grade horror film, "The Invasion of the Sportscar People." One wonders if anyone bothered to compute the total man-hours expended by Chevy Public relations types on these sorts of shots. The cars are 1955 models-- 1.3% of the entire model year build, in fact. (It was a slow year for sales, if not for performance-- the V-8 engine made its debut on the 1955 models).

Speaking of V-8s, a pair of early 'Vette examples are illustrated on the right. At the top of the page is the 1955 Chevy V-8 engine first announced for 1955. The engine pictured here is the standard Chevy unit. The Corvette version--dubbed the Turbo-Fire V-8--came with a different air cleaner and spiffier cosmetics, as well as 195 living, breathing horses. Chevy advertised the Turbo-Fire V-8 as "A Cyclone of Power," which it was, certainly when compared to the Blue Flame Six with one-third less power. An estimated 99% of the 1955 models were V-8s.

The engine shown at the bottom of the page is the landmark Corvette fuelie of 1957. Pontiac followed soon with its first Bonneville (in mid-year 1957) and Chrysler and Ford both experimented with units of their own. Most were trouble. The Ford and Chrysler units were touted for a short time, then quickly withdrawn and forgotten. The Pontiac unit--similar to Chevy's--failed to offer more power than the optional tri-carb set-up and so found few buyers.

manual shift transmissions. Indeed, this was an era in which sportscar enthusiasts heatedly debated whether a true sportscar could have wind-up windows, so pure Detroit-isms like automatic transmissions were clearly beyond the bounds of rational thought.

The engine--billed as the Blue Flame Six for Corvette purposes--was altered. The changes were not dramatic, just some easy "hotting up" of the sort backyard mechanics had been doing on their own for some time in a desperate attempt to breathe life into Chevy's moribund six-banger. Compression was raised to 8.0:1 (from 7.5:1 for the passenger cars), but more pep was needed still, so three (count 'em, three) carburetors were installed. Output was thus raised to a thoroughly unintoxicating 150 hp, giving the Corvette the dubious distinction of being America's most powerful six-cylinder engine.

This first 'Vette rode on a 102-inch wheelbase and tipped the scales at 2,705 pounds. By comparison, the contemporary Jaguar XK-120 weighed in at 2,912 pounds, though it had an infinitely more sophisticated engine rated at 160 hp and could easily beat the Corvette's 0 to 60 time of 11.2 seconds. Nevertheless, the Corvette was, in most respects, remarkably good for a first

Yet another group shot, below. These are 1957 models photographed in San Francisco.

14

American effort and it was priced at a relatively mild $3,498--more than $500 less than the Jag.

Chevrolet did not expect to sell many Corvettes that first year. Truth to tell, the project was undertaken as much for publicity reasons as anything else. Only 316 copies were built in 1953, but, the following year, a more substantial 3,640 units were produced.

There were no basic changes

Right, a 1956 Corvette.

made for 1954. A few minor accessories were made available and the choice of exterior colors was expanded by 300%, which is to say if the buyer did not like white--the only color available in 1953--he could, for 1954, order red, blue or black. He could also order a beige interior, in addition to the exclusive red of 1953, and a black top in addition to the former beige only. The Blue Flame Six engine was continued, but, in mid-year, a different camshaft upped the output to 155 hp. While the power enjoyed a modest increase, the price took a fairly dramatic drop to $2,774. That did not, however, include $178 for the mandatory standard Powerglide, but the real base price of $2,952 still represented a substantial cut and no doubt had a lot to do with the huge increase in sales.

The big news for Corvette came in 1955, though, when

Chevrolet's new V-8 engine was made available. As fitted in the Corvette, it developed a healthy 195 hp from its 265 cubic inches. The Corvette V-8 was listed at $2,909, while the six remained unchanged at $2,774. Powerglide was a genuine option now, as a 3-speed manual transmission was available as standard equipment. Most of the 1955 Corvettes were V-8 powered, but only 700 of all types were made. So why was the best Corvette yet a slug on the sales floor? The answer could be summed up in one word: Thunderbird.

In the early 1950s, Ford and Chevy were locked in mortal combat. Henry Ford II had taken over a stumbling Ford Motor Company in 1945 and was determined to re-establish it as the force to be reckoned with in the low-priced field. That meant a do or die struggle with Chevrolet and

15

Plymouth. Plymouth, on the wane itself at that time, was relatively easy pickings, but Chevrolet was a far tougher customer. Ford threw everything it had into the fight in the first few years after the war and, when that failed to install the Ford nameplate at the top of the sales charts, resorted to a brutal price war in 1953-54, which ultimately came to be known as the "Ford Blitz." It was in this environment that Chevy displayed its Corvette prototype and then announced limited production. Naturally Ford felt compelled to follow suit.

Ford's new Thunderbird arrived on the market during 1954, as a 1955 model. It had three big advantages over the Corvette.

First, the T-Bird was built of good old American steel, which made it seem less bizarre and, frankly, risky, than the 'Vette's off-the-wall fiberglass construction. The Thunderbird also had an excellent V-8 engine, specifically Ford's new-for-1954 overhead-valve job. Lastly, and more subtly, The Thunderbird was less an out-and-out sportscar than it was a luxury personal two-seater. It was more conventional and far more civilized, so, not surprisingly, it sold dramatically better: 16,155 were built during the 1955 model run, a 23 to 1 wipe-out. As a consequence, the Corvette was nearly squeezed into oblivion.

What saved the Corvette were two men: Ed Cole, Chevy's chief engineer and Zora Arkus-Duntov, Corvette's project manager. They were determined to develop the 'Vette into a true sportscar--something the Thunderbird clearly

One of the joys of doing research on a book such as this is that one gets to spend time sifting through the wonderful sort of black-and-white publicity stills public relations departments used to issue. Black-and-white was the film of choice and whereas the idea today seems to be to depict the car as objectively as possible, 1950s photographers often took a decidedly subjective point of view. They wanted to take photos that would make statements about the cars. These statements usually involved drama, sex, excitement, or any combination of the above. Sex was the most popular, of course, even with dowdy cars where the connection seemed ludicrous. The photo, right, of a 1958 'Vette clearly all makes sorts of statements, both blatant and subtle. Although obviously a studio shot, the car seems to be roaring right off the page. Significantly, we see only enough of the driver to know he is a man. Any man. Why not you? This could be your car. Your woman. Go for it!

16

was not--and one that could stand up to any competitor from any country. To do this, the car would have to be completely remade from the ground up.

For 1956, the Blue Flame Six was deleted and two 265 cid V-8's were offered, in 210 hp and 225 hp versions. The chassis underwent numerous refinements and the body was visibly altered for the first time. The headlights were positioned farther forward on the fenders, with no chrome stone

Left, the final assembly line during the 1958 model run.
Below, the interior of the Corvette in 1957.

guards. The front fenders and part of the doors had a concave section which became a Corvette trademark for several years to come. This section could be finished in a contrasting color. A choice of six body colors were now available.

In an effort to make the rather rudimentary 'Vette more competitive with the T-Bird, new options were offered, including power windows, an hydraulic folding top and an auxiliary hardtop. The $3,149 base price was nearly identical to the $3,151 base T-bird price, but the 1956 Corvette was clearly better targeted than before to the demands of the

marketplace. All these changes helped boost Corvette appeal and production rose to 3,467, nearly five times the previous year's total, while T-Bird production stagnated at 15,631. Ford was still dominant in the market, but all the growth was going to the Corvette, probably because many sportscar enthusiasts were giving the 'Vette serious consideration for the first time.

A significantly improved 1957 Corvette saw production increase by another 82% to 6,339 units. Thunderbird, in its last year as a two-seater, was also up, but only by 37%, so the Corvette continued to gain ground over its nemesis

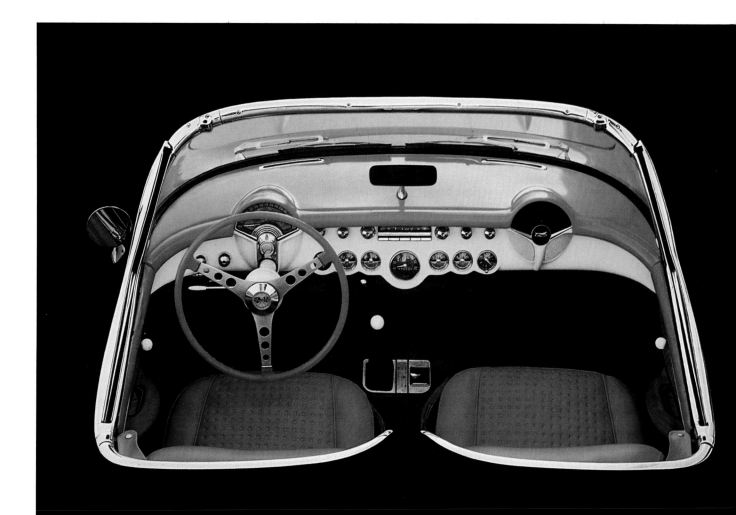

from Dearborn.

Corvette styling remained unchanged for 1957. Lots of changes, though, were to be found under the hood. The standard engine was a beefy 220 hp single-carb version of the larger, 283 cid V-8. Two 4-barrel carburetors were available to develop 245 hp for $140, or 270 hp for $170. The really big news, though, was fuel-injection, which was added to the option list and gave the Corvette the distinction of being the first American-built car so equipped. The sign of Zora, once again. A 250 hp fuel-injected 283 V-8 was a $450 option and, for $675, a 283 hp fuel-injected version was offered. That meant a Corvette could be had off the showroom floor with an engine that developed 1 hp for each cubic inch of displacement.

This was quite a remarkable achievement in 1957, even though the Chrysler 300-B had cracked that barrier the year before with its

RAMJET FUEL INJECTION—
unsurpassed performance!

This motoring *first* gives you instantaneous throttle response, greater power, faster warm-ups and greater overall fuel savings. Fuel is pressure-injected directly at each cylinder intake port, eliminating the carburetor entirely! Optional at extra cost with Powerglide, or 3-speed or 4-speed Synchro-Mesh transmission.

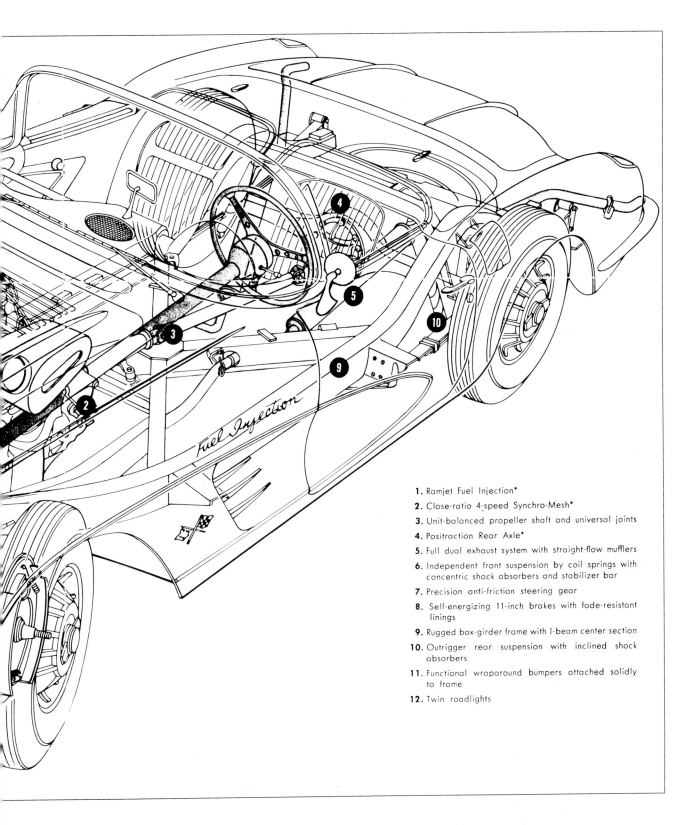

1. Ramjet Fuel Injection*
2. Close-ratio 4-speed Synchro-Mesh*
3. Unit-balanced propeller shaft and universal joints
4. Positraction Rear Axle*
5. Full dual exhaust system with straight-flow mufflers
6. Independent front suspension by coil springs with concentric shock absorbers and stabilizer bar
7. Precision anti-friction steering gear
8. Self-energizing 11-inch brakes with fade-resistant linings
9. Rugged box-girder frame with I-beam center section
10. Outrigger rear suspension with inclined shock absorbers
11. Functional wraparound bumpers attached solidly to frame
12. Twin roadlights

Left, a photo of the 1959 'Vette (don't let the license plate fool you).

Above, a showroom brochure cutaway of the 1958 'Vette showing various features.

optional engine (a rude fact tactfully overlooked by Chevrolet's advertising mavens). On the other hand, the Chrysler 300-B was an enormous car compared to a Corvette and it

could be reasonably argued that it was in the 'Vette that this feat was first translated into raw, spine-snapping performance. Tom McCahill reported in *Mechanix Illustrated* that a 283 hp manual

Above, a modern-day shot of a 1959 Corvette with its detachable hardtop. This photograph contrasts sharply in style with the photo on the pages 16-17. No sex, no speed, little drama. Subtelty is the watchword here, in both color and format.

to Corvette since Zora Arkus-Duntov was Ford's decision to add two more seats to the Thunderbird in 1958, thus abandoning the sportscar market to Chevrolet. Despite the fact that the T-Bird had been the market leader and had increased its sales every year, Ford marketeers wanted an even bigger market for their feathered friend. A direct result of that move was that in 1958--a recession year--Corvette set a new production record of 9,168 units, up 45%. In fact, Corvette, Thunderbird and Rambler were just about the only domestics to post sales gains that year.

For 1958, Corvette's one standard and four optional engines continued, but power ratings were up to 230 hp at the bottom and 290 hp in the most potent of the fuel-injected versions. Either fuel-injected engine cost $484 extra. Meanwhile, Corvette's base price had climbed to $3,631.

Styling was altered slightly for 1958. Dual headlights were deemed a fashion necessity, the grille was revised, and the front bumper made more practical. Fake louvers ran across the rear of the hood and the front part of the side coves were filled with a convex stainless steel section. Two Chrome stripes ran down the rear deck. Inside, a totally new

† Just for the record, The 1956 Chrysler 300-B listed its standard 354 cid engine at 340 hp with a 9.0:1 compression ratio. The optional engine, with 10.0:1 compression, was rated at 355 hp. Thirty years after the fact it is hard to say how reliable any of these claims actually were. There was a horsepower war going on and some of the most amazing engineering of the era was done by advertising writers.

shift Corvette he drove tested out to 0 to 60 in 6.2 seconds and reached a top speed of around 140 mph. Literally, Corvette was

away to the races. In fact, Heavy Duty Racing Suspension was a $725 option.†

The best thing that happened

instrument panel appeared.

Some of these styling excesses were eliminated for 1959, notably the fake louvers and the rear deck chrome. The fender cove fillers were now painted. Production increased to 9,670, while standard and optional engine choices and power remained unchanged. *Sports Cars llustrated* got a 0 to 60 time of 6.6 seconds in a 290 hp Corvette with 4-speed stick. Their standing start quarter-mile time was 14.9 seconds, ending at 98 mph

With the 1960 Corvette, power was increased for the three most potent optional engines. The

Above, 1961, and below, 1962 Corvettes.

most powerful carbureted engine developed 270 hp, while the fuel-injected engines were increased to 275 and 315 hp. To better handle the increased power, only the 3- or 4-speed manual transmissions could be ordered with fuel-injection. Production rose yet again in 1960, reaching 10,261 units, then went up again, to 10,939 units, for 1961, despite a price increase from $3,872 to $3,934.

Engines remained virtually the same in 1961, but styling was significantly modified. Up front, the center grille cavity gave up its teeth for a chrome mesh pattern. The most notable alteration in 1961, however, was the new rear end shape. This was the first real body change since 1956 and garnered quite a bit of attention at the time--much of it unfavorable. The new styling, obviously (in retrospect) a precursor of the 1963 Sting Ray, struck many observers as an awkward graft onto the existing Corvette body. The new design did allow for multiple round taillights, something of a Chevy design signature at this time, but the built-in exhaust outlets were deleted.

Virtually no change was made to the rear of the 1962 model. The grille, however, was blacked out and the side coves lost their chrome edging. New chrome trim was placed on the fake vent in the coves.

If styling was on hold in 1962, performance was not. The engines were drastically altered for the 1962 Corvettes. Most importantly, they were all increased in displacement to 327 cubic inches. The base engine put out 250 hp. For $54 extra, a 300 hp version was offered, or $108 could get you 340 hp. Fuel-injection continued to be listed at $484, but only in one version rated at 360 hp.

Production continued to soar, rising from 10,939 units in 1961 to 14,531 for 1962. Bigger things were in the wings, though, for 1963. The Corvette was about to come of age.

Chapter Two
THE STING OF THE RAY

The first decade of the Corvette story was one of continual refinements and improvements. In the process, virtually nothing about the car was left untouched, but the changes had been evolutionary rather than revolutionary. So, while the original 'Vette and the 1962 model were, for all practical purposes two completely different automobiles, the Corvette had been transformed one part at a time from the basic platform and body shell that had first entered production in 1953. The revolution arrived with the 1963 Sting Rays.

The 1963 Sting Ray represented an entirely new Corvette platform and body shell, while the chassis and drivetrain was developed from the previous

On these two pages, the 1963 Sting Ray coupe. The man is Zora Arkus-Duntov.

Above, 1966 Corvettes moving down the assembly line.

models. Totally different in appearance, the new Corvette none-the-less revived two styling features of the past: It had hidden headlights and the sport coupe used a fastback shape similar to one that had first appeared on one of the 1953 GM Motorama Corvette variants, and more than a little reminiscent of the boattail designs of the classic era. Bill Mitchell,

GM's styling czar loved the boattail and put it on a number of GM cars, most notably the 1963 Sting Ray and the 1971 Riviera. On the Riv' it was a disaster owing to the sheer size of the car. With the far smaller Sting Ray, however, it was pure genius. The only feature of the 1963 Sting Ray that caused complaints was the split rear window. The center divider was

deleted for 1964. Unlike, previous models, though, the Sting Ray coupe sported a fixed top, not an add-on top for the convertible body style.

The convertible's base price was down one dollar to $4,037, and the sport coupe listed for

$4,257. An auxiliary hardtop was still available for the convertible, as well, at a cost of an extra $237. Extra cost of fuel-injection was down a bit to $480. Major specifications for all engines were unchanged for 1963.

Disc brakes were offered for the first time, installed on all four wheels, while drum brakes were available on a delete credit basis. Even though disc brakes became standard, the base price held constant. Production in 1963 saw a jump to 21,513. That was almost evenly divided between roadsters and sport coupes.

Below, the 1965 coupe.

Except for the removal of the fake chrome hood vents and the center divider in the rear window of the sport coupe, appearance for 1964 remained the same. Power, on the other hand, was increased in the two most powerful motors for 1964, to 365 and 375 hp, respectively.

Production was also up, although just a smidgen to 22,229. Despite this, the coupe fell in popularity, accounting for about 37 percent of production. Coupes declined again for 1965, even though total production rose marginally to 23,562 during that model run.

The 1965 models were the

beneficiaries for still more refinements. A change from two horizontal fender depressions to three vertical functional louvers coincided with some engine changes. No fewer than six engines were offered for the 1965 Corvette. A 350 hp 327 V-8 was added to the powerplants of the previous year. Then, in mid-season, a 425 hp 396 cubic inch V-8 made its appearance. *Road & Track's* test of the 375 hp fuel-injected Corvette recorded a 0 to 60 time of 6.3 seconds and a quarter mile acceleration time of 14.6 seconds at 98 mph.

Engine choices dropped to four for the 1966 model. The two 327

V-8s came in 300 hp and 350 hp editions. The 396 cid V-8 was replaced by two versions of a 427 cubic inch V-8, rated at 390 hp and 425 hp. A specially marked hood indicated the 427-powered models and fuel-injection was no longer offered. Production for 1966 increased to 27,720, with coupes accounting for about 36 percent.

The Sting Ray was supposed to be retired at the end of the 1966 model run so that it could be replaced with a dramatically new body for 1967. Production problems caused a last-minute delay in the program, however, and the 1966 model was continued over for 1967 with a few modifications here and there. The existence of the new model was well known to enthusiasts, though, and many of them preferred to wait out the delay before plunking down their cash.

As a consequence, for the first time in 12 years Corvette production declined from the preceding year.

There were 22,940 1967 model Corvettes built. They were identifiable principally by their five fender vents. Powerwise, it was back to six engine choices. A 400 hp edition of the 427 V-8 was added, as well as a hot 430 hp version.

The highest rated V-8 was a $437, 435 hp mill. *Car and Driver* tested a Corvette with this engine, and got a 0 to 60 time of 4.7 seconds, and the quarter mile in 13.6 seconds at 104 mph. The 430 hp motor was a $948 racing engine that reportedly developed some 560 hp. Only 20 were said to have been installed, however.

Above, the 1967 427 engine and, right, the 1967 coupe.

32

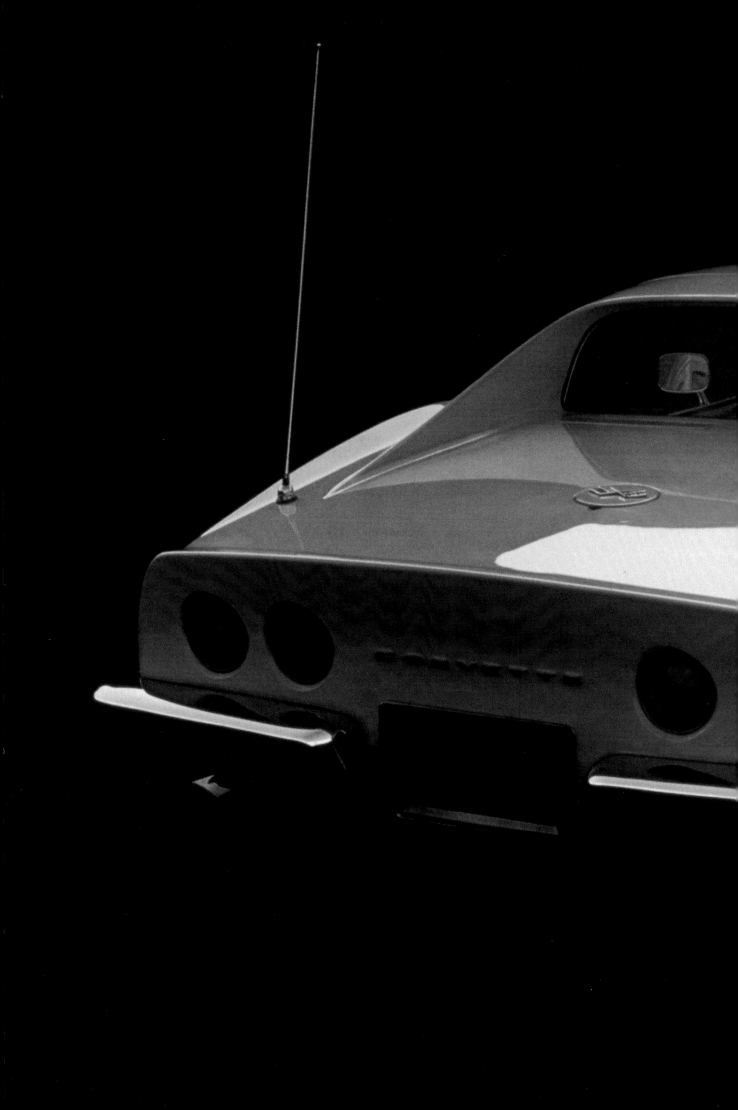

Chapter Three
THE LEGEND IN ITS PRIME

It took 10 years for the Corvette to get its first new body in 1963. The Corvette's third new body appeared in only five more years, on the 1968 models. The 1968 series was, by any standard, the most successful in Corvette history. It lasted longer and sold better than any Corvette series before or since, and, in the minds of millions of enthusiasts, became the personification of what the Corvette represents.

The 1963 series Sting Ray was a radical departure from what had gone before. The 1968 series was both a continuation of the Sting Ray and a revolutionary modernization of the themes it represented. Many at the time thought the new design was too radical, too glitzy. Over the succeeding 15 years, however, it withstood the test of time. If the shock value of the 1968 series was lost in the interim, the brilliance of the concept behind it was not. The 1968 Sting Ray was the spirit of dynamic motion represented in fiberglass and steel.

The 1968 coupe featured detachable rear window and roof panels, but a detachable hardtop continued to be offered on the convertible. Prices went up from $4,241 to $4,320 for the convertible, and $4,388 to $4,663 for the coupe. Production jumped to 28,566. Coupes, as they had in the past, continued to account for about 35 percent of the total production. Engines remained basically the same despite the new body and interior. *Motor Trend* tested a 435 hp model, getting from 0 to 60 in 6.3 seconds and recording a quarter mile in 14.1 seconds at 103 mph.

Changes to the 1969 model were limited. Essentially the 1969 Corvette was a continuation of the dramatically successful 1968 edition. News with engines included an increase in displacement from 327 to 350 cubic inches. However, these new displacements retained the 300 hp standard and 350 hp optional output ratings. Other optional engines were 427 cubers rated at 390 hp, 400 hp and three different ones rated at 435 hp (including the racing edition). Using a street version 427, *Road & Track* found 0 to 60 to take 6.1 seconds and the quarter mile 14.3 seconds at 98

Right, an early publicity shot of the 1968 convertible shows the extraordinary lines of the new car.

mph.

Although there was very little appearance change in 1969, production shot up to 38,762. Equally surprising, the percentage of coupes suddenly hit 57 percent. Prices were raised to $4,438 and $4,781 for the convertible and coupe, respectively.

The Corvette was little changed for 1970. Square mesh grillwork and a square grille design on the fender vents appeared on these models. Engine changes for 1970 were more extensive. This model saw the addition of a 370 hp version of the 350 cid V-8. The 427 V-8 was replaced by a 454 cubic inch engine monster in 390 hp and 465 hp versions. The latter was the most powerful Corvette

Above, 1968 coupe interior. The exterior design of the third generation 'Vette deservedly gets tremendous attention, but the interior was a work of art, too. Below, 1969 coupe.

38

street engine ever offered. *Road & Track* tested the 390 hp 454 with 3-speed automatic. The results were 0 to 60 in 7.0 seconds and a quarter mile in 15.0 seconds at 93 mph. If those seem just a bit disappointing, it must be borne in mind that the Corvette now weighed 3,740 pounds. It was no longer a lightweight.

The nation suffered a recession in 1970, and, probably as a consequence, the Corvette suffered a sudden 55 percent fall in production. A total of 17,316 'Vettes saw the light of day in 1970. Coupes rose to 62 percent of that smaller total.

Government exhaust emission standards were also beginning to restrict engine performance at this time. As a consequence, 1971

models had lower power ratings. The 350 V-8s were listed as 270 hp and 330 hp, while the two 454s were 365 hp and 425 hp. *Car and Driver* tested all four Corvettes for a comparison. As expected, the 425 hp engine gave the best results: 0 to 60 in 5.3 seconds, a quarter mile in 13.8 seconds at 104.65 mph and top speed of 152 mph. Interestingly, the more potent of the 454 engines gave better fuel mileage (9 to 14 mpg) than the lesser 454 (8 to 11 mpg).

With little change in

Above, 1971 coupe.
Below, 1970 convertible. This shot was the recipient of skillful airbrushing. An earlier version of this same photo showed the car with 1969 style fender vents.

appearance, the 1972 Corvette had just three engine choices, the fewest since 1956. The standard 350 was offered in 200 hp and 255 hp ratings, and the 454 (not sold in California) came only in a 270 hp version. Also worth noting: 1971 models had lower quoted power ratings due to the fact that the industry changed from gross to net ratings for horsepower. *Motor Trend* tests resulted in the following for the 200 hp 255 hp and 270 hp engines, respectively: 0 to 60 in 8.5, 6.9 and 6.8 seconds; quarter mile in 15.2 at 83, 14.3 at 92 and 14.1 seconds at 93 mph; and fuel consumption of 10-14, 9-12 and 13-15 mpg.

But, as performance in 1972 fell, prices rose: from $5,259 to $5,496 for the convertible, and $5,496 to $5,533 for the coupe.

Production rebounded to 21,801 for 1971, and 27,004 for 1972. The coupe's share of overall production had risen to over 75 percent.

Although the same body continued over for 1973, there were numerous noticeable changes. New Federal bumper regulations were a problem and were neatly incorporated into the design. The Corvette did not use a chrome finish, but, rather, used body-color bumpers for the first time. Also that year, a single large functional fender vent appeared and the rear window was no longer removable.

If the decline of the great American performance machine was in doubt, the ratings of the Corvette engines in 1973 were depressing news. Federalizing of the 350 engine resulted in 190 hp

and 250 hp ratings. Oddly, the 454 was upgraded to 275 hp and available everywhere, California included.

Car and Driver found performance slightly better, however. Further good news was available. In a 1974 comparison with Ferrari, Jaguar, Mercedes and Porsche, *Road & Track* found the 250 hp Corvette the fastest in both 0 to 60 in 7.4 seconds and the quarter mile in 15.8 at 124 mph. So, it seemed that although horsepower ratings were in flux, Corvette was somehow still able to maintain the standards enthusiasts had come to expect of it.

The 250 hp engine was the only unchanged motor for 1974. The base 350 was rated at 195 hp, up 5. The only 454 engine was, however, downrated by 5 hp to 270 hp. Despite hampered horsepower and a gasoline shortage, Corvette production continued to rise: from 30,464 in 1973 to a whopping 37,502 in 1974. This was particularly remarkable. The Arab Oil Embargo had sent shock waves through American society. For the first time in our nation's history, Americans felt vulnerable to outside forces. It was not a good feeling. In general, economy cars were in sudden, tremendous demand. It was widely predicted that big-engined, high performance cars were doomed-- dinosaurs waiting for official notice of their extinction. Perhaps it was a fear that cars such as the Corvette would no longer be available that spurred sales, but the few remaining high performance cars on the American market similar to the 'Vette (the Pontiac

Trans Am, for example) suddenly rose in sales. Corvette coupe production, for its part, climbed to 85 percent of the total.

Prices were climbing, too, in 1974. Convertible and coupe base prices rose from $5,399 and

Above, a 1972 Corvette convertible at the country club.

developed a mere 165 hp, with 205 hp optional. *Motor Trend* found the 165 hp Corvette could only do 0 to 60 in 9.55 seconds, and a quarter mile in 16.43 seconds at 87.54 mph. Gas mileage, however, had risen to 16.5 mpg, and that was important to car buyers in 1975.

Worse news for Corvette enthusiasts was in store. The power rating in the base 1976 engine plummeted to just 180 hp. The optional version, on the other hand, was up a bit to 210 hp. *Road & Track* found the latter could do 0 to 60 in 8.1 seconds and a quarter mile in 16.5 seconds at 87 mph. The coupe was $6,810 in 1975 and jumped to $7,605 for 1976. The last Corvette convertible, priced at $6,558, was a 1975 model, of which just 4,629 were made out of a total build of 38,465. Model production in 1976 reached 46,558 units.

Styling changed very little for 1975 and 1976.

The sameness was due to continue a while longer. Except for a new console, there was hardly any change for 1977, either. Even the engine compartment saw virtually no alterations. A milestone was marked on March 14th, however, when the 500,000th Corvette drove off the St. Louis assembly line.

The following model year saw another milestone. Corvette's 25th anniversary was celebrated in 1978 with the offering of a Silver Anniversary paint option. It had a two-tone, light silver-over dark silver finish that cost $399 extra. Also, in recognition of its quarter century, the Corvette was chosen as the pace car for the Indianapolis

$5,562 in 1973, respectively, to $5,766 and $6,002 in 1974. The greatest appearance change for 1974 was the hidden rear bumper--an aluminum bar covered with a

layer of body color urethane.

Very little external change occurred on the 1975 models. Under the hood, only the 350 V-8 was used. In base form, it

500. The Limited Edition Pace Car, a separate model, was produced. Among other features, it was painted black over silver. There were 6,502 produced and priced at an absurd $13,654. A speculator's market in these already over-priced cars ensued and saw the going price reach $20,000, or even higher. It did not last. The standard price, up sharply from $8,648 in 1977, was a substantial $9,382. Total 1978 production was 46,776, down from the 49,213 of 1977.

The most noticeable external change for 1978 was the fastback rear window. Engine power rose slightly to 185 hp and 220 hp.

Performance improved, as noted by *Road & Track's* test of the 220 hp model: 0 to 60 took just 6.5 seconds and the quarter mile, 15.2 seconds at 95 mph. They reported normal driving fuel consumption of 15 mpg.

Car and Driver's test of the 1979 model, with optional 225 hp engine, produced a 0 to 60 time of 6.6 seconds, a quarter mile time of 15.3 seconds and a top speed of 127 mph. Their fuel consumption was 14 mpg in either city or country. The optional V-8 was rated at 225 hp and the base engine was 195 hp, up 5 and 10 hp, respectively.

Up also were the prices: $10,220 for 1979 and $13,140 for 1980. But the hefty hike included air-conditioning, adjustable steering wheel and power windows, among other items. Production set a record-high in the 1979 model year of 53,807, but

Below, a 1974 coupe showing the body-color urethane bumpers fore and aft that were standard for the first time that year. This model marked the most significant change yet in the 1968 series 'Vettes. It also proved that skillful designers can improve on a winner.

Right, 1975 coupe.

fell back to just 40,614 for 1980. Once again, a national recession was primarily responsible for a decline in Corvette production.

In 1980, there were styling revisions to the front end and a spoiler built into the rear. Power dropped 5 hp in the base engine and rose 5 hp in the optional engine. The standard 190 hp motor was not available in California, however. Instead, a 305 cid 180 hp V-8 was exclusive to that state. For 1981, just one engine was available everywhere. It was the 190 hp 350 V-8.

There was a change in venue in 1981. From the beginning, Corvette's had been built in St. Louis. In 1981, production was relocated from to a new plant in Bowling Green, Kentucky. In all, there were 40,606 Corvettes built during the 1981 season. Although that was about the same as 1980, production fell to 25,407 for 1982 in anticipation of the all-new 1983

(later to become 1984) model. The 1981 Corvette was priced at $16,259, but, for 1982, the price went up to $18,290.

Black rocker panels marked the 1981 models, while the 1982s were identifiable by the "cross-fire injection" script on the front fenders. That indicated the reintroduction of fuel-injection. This particular unit was a new computer-controlled throttle body injection system that raised the output to 200 hp. *Car and Driver* put one of these models through its paces, getting a 0 to 60 time of 8.1 seconds, a quarter mile in 15.9 seconds at 86 mph and fuel economy fell to 14 mpg.

In view of Corvette's closing era in 1982, a Collector Edition was offered. There were 6,759 built. Among its features were special aluminum wheels, a lift-open rear window and silver/beige metallic paint. Price was a substantial $22,538.

45

Above left, a pair of 1976 'Vettes in a western setting.

Below right, the Corvette Indy 500 Pace Car with a few luminaries, present and future. The man at the driver's door is then Chevrolet general manager, Robert D. Lund. The tall man at the rear of the car was then Chevrolet's chief engineer. Within a few months, he would become general manager of Pontiac, then Chevrolet and, eventually, after several other assignments, president of GM. His name: Robert C. Stempel.

The first generation Corvette styling had been substantially reworked twice--in 1956 and in 1961. The second generation Corvette had gone largely unchanged during its run, but had lasted only five model years and the fifth year, 1967, was a fluke caused by the unexpected delay of the third generation cars. When the third generation appeared in 1968, it confounded all observers by lasting essentially unchanged for a decade-and-a-half. Why such a lengthy run for the third series? The reasons were several.

In the first place, the Corvette announced to the public for 1968 was an enormously successful car from virtually every standpoint. There were, however, other, more complex factors at work.

Leadership at Chevy was in crisis in the early 1970s, the time during which a fourth generation model should have been in gestation. The crisis revolved around John DeLorean, then Chevrolet's controversial general

manager. He was forced to resign from GM in September, 1972, under circumstances that have never been fully explained. He was succeeded by F. James MacDonald, another Pontiac alumnus who was later to become president of GM. MacDonald was not, however, a "product" man and the confusion at Chevy concerning product strategy grew more serious during his tenure.

A final note of confusion was

Left, 1977 and 1979 coupes. Below, 1982 hatchbacks.

caused by the Arab Oil Embargo, in the winter of 1973-74, which prompted the Federal Government to insert itself "whole hog" into the affairs of the auto industry. Suddenly Big Brother was peering over the shoulder of every engineer in Motown. The frustration was especially intense among those responsible for high performance machines such as the Corvette.

For a time it was thought there might not even be a fourth generation Corvette. After a number of false starts, however, the fourth generation appeared in

the spring of 1983 as a 1984 model. Oddly, there was no 1983 model designated as such. The 1982 models were continued until the factory shut down to change-over to the 1984s. The original intention had been to designate the new cars as 1983 models and some promotional items were designed with that designation, but the introduction came so late in the 1983 model year that it was decided to skip right to 1984. It was just one final bit of confusion surrounding the story of the third generation Corvettes.

Chapter Four
THE PROMISE IS KEPT

The 1984 Corvette was probably the most eagerly awaited new model in that line's history. The tension was all the more palpable because of the repeated delays in the project. The 1984 Corvette had been rumored to be imminent since at least the mid-1970s. Talk of the introduction occurred as frequently as talk of the next Beatles' reunion--and with just as much accuracy. When the go-ahead was finally given for actual production, the project was still delayed from 1982 to 1983. Even then, it came so late in the 1983 model year that the new car was termed a 1984, leading to the curious situation in which a model year was officially skipped although there was no suspension in actual production.

The 1984 Corvette was an amazing example of how completely an American car could hold to its orignal concept, despite changes in the industry, economy and public tastes. Another amazing fact in today's mixed-up world: All Corvette engines have been Chevrolet-built.

The 1984 model was completely restyled, yet retained enough of the traditional image to be unmistakably Corvette. The 1968 series had been criticized in some quarters for its glitzy, boy-racer styling. By contrast, the new car was clean and functional from stem to stern. The new body, still fiberglass, rode on a 96.2-inch wheelbase chassis, and was 176.5 inches long--shorter by about two inches and nine inches, respectively. There was a 178-pound weight reduction to 3,164, but price was not reduced. It jumped, officially, from $18,290 to $21,800, but by more like $10,000 in practice. Still, Chevy dealers were unable to keep them in stock at seemingly any price.

Handling was a revelation. The new 'Vette redefined roadability in American automobiles, even though it was criticized for unnecessary harshness by many auto writers.

Left, the business end of the 1984 Corvette.

And, the new car was fast. The 350 V-8 was rated at 205 hp. Car and Driver's test yielded a 0 to 60 time of 6.7 seconds, a quarter mile in 15.2 seconds at 90 mph and a top speed of 138 mph. The optional transmission was a remarkable automatic overdrive unit that, in effect, added three optional overdrive gears to the standard Corvette 4-speed manual shift transmission.

With negligible visual difference, the 1985 Corvette was a refined version of the pace-setting 1984. A softer standard suspension featuring gas-cell shocks made the vehicle a bit more civilized, while tuned-port fuel injection added to both horsepower and torque. The 5.7 liter engine was now rated at 230 hp. According to *Road & Track*, that gave it a 0 to 60 time of 6.6 seconds and a quarter mile time of 15.0 seconds at 91 mph. Fuel consumption in normal driving was estimated at 19 mpg. Brakes and transmission components were all beefed up.

The 1986 Corvette was an improved version of the 1985, although the really big news was the mid-year addition of a convertible to the line. Mechanically, the big story was the addition to the standard equipment list of anti-lock brakes. A new theft-deterrent system, called VATS (Vehicle Anti-Theft System), was added in an attempt to cut the daunting rate of Corvette thefts nationwide. VATS augmented the previously standard GM anti-theft system by adding coding features that would disable the ignition if the wrong key was

used or if the normal ignition system was bypassed. It apparently works, because Corvette thefts have taken a substantial drop as of this writing, although they remain a serious problem.

The 1987 Corvette was little altered and, for 1988, changes were mostly limited to new colors, wheels and tires. This has, however, just been the calm before the storm for, in 1989, truly extraordinary developments have taken place. America's first production 6-speed manual transmission and selective ride control are the least of the

Above, the 1984 interior.

developments, although in normal times, they would be considered front page news.

The 6-speed manual was designed jointly by Germany's ZF and Corvette engineers, replacing the old 4+3 manual overdrive. Computer-aided gear selection (CAGS) mode is designed to optimize fuel economy and reduce engine RPMs by automatically directing shifts from 1st to 4th gears under light acceleration conditions. Just step on the gas and you'll shift through the gears. A "one-to-four" indicator light

appears on the intrument panel cluster under the tachometer when the CAGS mode is engaged. The 4-speed automatic overdrive transmission continues as a no-cost option.

Delco Bilstein Selective Ride Control is an innovative suspension option available exclusively on the 1989 Corvette coupe with the Z51 performance handling option and the 6-speed manual transmission. A switch position permits the driver to select six different shock absorber damping levels depending on vehicle speed.

The really big news for 1989,

however, is the Corvette ZR1, the so-called "King of the Hill" model, featuring the fabulous LT5 engine. The LT5 is one of the very few four-cam, four-valve-per-cylinder V-8 engines to be built anywhere in the world for anything other than all-out racing competition. It is the first all-aluminum production engine of this type manufactured in the United States and combines an unusual blend of dedicated high-performance design with long-term durability and a high degree of fuel economy.

The LT5 engine was designed and developed by General Motors'

Group Lotus Division in Hethel, England, in conjunction with CPC (Chevrolet-Pontiac-GM Canada) Engineering which provided concept direction and much design input throughout the process. It is being manufactured under contract by Mercury Marine in Stillwater, Oklahoma.

The relatively low volume and highly specialized manufacturing process of this engine program made the Stillwater facility an ideal choice. This is where Mercury produces its Mercruiser stern drive and inboard engines, many of which are based on marine conversions of standard GM automotive engines.

GM and Mercury have had an association of technical and manufacturing collaboration going back to the start of Mercury itself. A world leader in highly engineered aluminum castings, Mercury also makes extensive use of high precision machining of mating aluminum surfaces using gasketless anerobic sealing, one of the design features of the LT5 engine.

Mercury contracts out much of the foundry work, but more than 95 percent of the highly specialized machining is done in-house. This takes place in a special area in its facility utilizing computer-controlled flexible machining centers. Final assembly is carried out at a series of work stations on two parallel lines in an area closed off from the rest of the Stillwater facility to maintain a

Following pages, a sampling of Corvettes down through the years, from 1953 to 1984.

53

clean environment. Operating like an engine-building shop, the engines are assembled by hand.

"We knew, back in April of 1985 when we began looking at the LT5, that each and every one of our objectives was going to be a tough bogey to meet†," says Chevrolet's chief engineer Fred Schaafsma "Only by technological breakthroughs could we redefine the economy and acceleration relationship enough in our favor to accomplish all of our corporate goals."

"And that's why we're so excited

†See page 5 for a complete listing.

about the LT5 because it really does represent some pretty impressive advances, not only in high-performance engine design, but in manufacturing and production technology as well."

Predating the Lotus/GM meeting and prior to any hard specifications for what was to become the LT5 engine, some very interesting vehicles appeared on the Corvette Group's testing schedules--turbocharged V-6s, twin turbocharged V-8s and 600 hp normally aspirated V-8s. All tested during the early 1980s.

Out of these test programs came a long list of what the group

Above, 1989 convertible.

didn't like--and a short list of what they did. The turbocharged V-6 program was dismissed due to its NVH (noise, vibration and harshness) profile.

Corvette Chief Dave McLellan felt the 90° Turbo V-6 program clearly established the need (at any expense, even including a longer wheelbase) to accommodate a V-8 for its inherent smoothness and tractability.

One program which initially had considerable internal support was the twin turbo V-8. Fourteen of these cars were built and went through extensive testing before the project was shelved. The general conclusion was that they were emmissions and fuel inefficient and, more importantly, not cutting edge technology.

One important philosophy which evolved from these test programs was the concept of a Bi-Modal vehicle--Bi-Modal in that it is two cars in one.

When the driver is in a "civilian" mode, the car accommodates him in every respect--quiet, docile, smooth, totally unobtrusive and non-demanding.

On demand, however, it transports its driver to whatever performance level is required, offering the speed, precision and response of all but pure race cars.

Equally important, the

Below, 1988 coupe.

transition from one mode to the other is quite linear and predictable with no surprises for the driver.

The performance potential of the LT5-equipped Corvette ZR1 will be quite astounding, not all of which will be directed at blazing speed. The inherent safety features are equally impressive and include braking and cornering power in excess of 1 g.

While the LT5 engine shares many features with Chevrolet's Indy V-8 racing engine, it has smooth, torquey low-speed characteristics not unlike the standard Corvette 5.7 liter (350 cid) V-8. The LT5 also displaces 5.7 liters and, despite the increase in bulk normally associated with four-cam engines, its is so compact it fits into the same space as the standard central cam pushrod L98. This is accomplished through some

creative package design with only minimal changes to the firewall.

The existing pushrod L98 engine is itself a highly refined development of the classic small-block Chevy and the new LT5 shares its 4.40 inch cylinder bore spacing. In order to find room for the LT5's aluminum cylinder liners, however, the bore has been reduced to a diameter of 3.90 inches, bringing the stroke to 3.66 inches in order to maintain the 5.7 liter displacement. This slightly raises the block deck height as compared to standard engine which has a 4.00 inch bore and 3.48 inch stroke. A narrow included angle (22°) between the valves and placement of the head bolts under the camshafts also contributes to the engine's compact size by allowing the cylinder heads to be unusually narrow for this type of design.

Each pair of camshafts topping the heads is driven by a duplex roller chain instead of the expected Gilmer (cog) belt with its much larger pulleys. This allows the engine to be physically smaller so the Corvette's hoodline can remain unaltered. Some external accessories and components are grouped between the cylinder block valley and the bottom of the plenum chamber.

At the front of the engine, both the alternator and air conditioning compressor are mounted in this space and along with the power steering pump are driven with a single serpentine belt of the type introduced on the 1984 Corvette. This belt also drives the water pump which, while located in a familiar spot above the crank pulley, now mounts directly to the cast aluminum front cover. This cover also forms the back of the water pump housing and

Some readers may have noticed the non-standard amber taillights on the ZR1 which graces our cover. Above and right, the actual 1989 ZR1 in California (James R. Moody photographs).

incorporates internal water passages. The rear portion of this space is used to full advantage with the ignition module mounted directly over a specially designed Delco Remy-Nippendenso gear

reduction starter which fills the rear portion of the block valley. This starter location leaves the lower sides of the crankcase clear, allowing large catalytic converters to be incorporated into the tubular exhaust manifolds. The individual primary pipes exhaust directly into these converters, greatly reducing heat loss causing the catalyst to react quickly with maximum effectiveness.

The LT5's tremendous top-end horsepower, combined with extreme low-speed flexibility and good fuel mileage, is made possible by a unique three-phase induction system. The intake plenum chamber looks superficially similar to the pushrod L98, except that the throttle body has three butterflies instead of two, and there are now 16 runners instead of eight. These runners feed air directly into each of the injector housings which have an electronically controlled sequentially fired fuel injector

targeted over each of the intake valves.

Within each cylinder, the intake ports, valves and cam lobes are divided into two groups, the primary being the one toward the front of the engine and secondary to the rear. The secondary ports are slightly larger in diameter and contain a port throttle butterfly which is actuated through a mechanical linkage by a vacuum diaphragm which is signaled by the computer.

The power "Valet" switch that is located on the center console limits engine output when in the normal position by preventing the secondary port throttle valves from operating. In this mode, the engine breathes through the primary ports only, so that operation, in effect, is on three valves per cylinder. The secondary intake valve is also moving but admits no fuel-air mixture.

Below half-throttle--or 3500 RPM--things are as they were.

injectors come on-line. At this point things really begin to happen, with the engine now running on all 16 injectors and all 32 valves.

The secondary intake valves, which are now admitting fuel-air mixture to the cylinders, are actuated by cam lobes which have more duration than the primaries. The effect is to produce true variable valve timing, optimizing flow and producing both tractable low speed and impressive high speed engine characteristics in a single engine. In order to maintain an attractive, durable and low-maintenance appearance, the entire

But, when the driver's foot goes to the floor, the secondary port throttle valves open to permit fuel-air mixture to enter the secondary intake valves. The secondary port throttles open in a similar manner as secondaries on a four-barrel carburetor and the eight secondary

Above, 1989 LT5 engine (James R. Moody photograph).
Below, Corvette/ZF S6-40 six-speed manual transmission.
Right, 1989 LT5 engine.

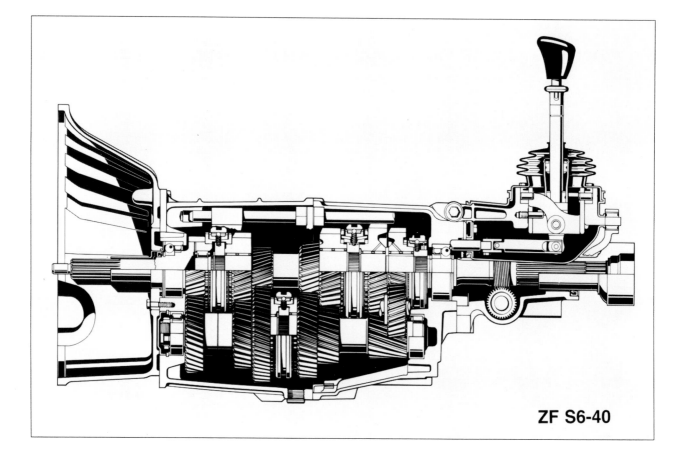

ZF S6-40

system is aridited and silver powder-coated before assembly.

The intricate cast aluminum cylinder heads have insert valve guides and seats. Their twin camshafts are retained directly by the cam covers. A spark plug is centrally located between the four valves of each cylinder which have an included angle of 22 degrees. This provides a shallow open combustion chamber and allows good straight port geometry and fuel squish area.

The intake ports are individual, with the secondary port throttle linkage facing down towards the block valley. The exhaust ports are divided most of the way out, but are siamesed at the exhaust flange. The valves are operated through direct-acting hydraulic lifters which eliminate any need for supplemental adjusting fingers, dashpots or other linkage which unnecessarily add to valve train inertia.

The cams are driven by an inverted tooth primary chain which drives a half-speed idler located in front of a roller chain sprocket on a common hub. This double-row roller chain directly drives the four cam sprockets and is kept in constant adjustment by hydraulic tensioners on the slack side of each chain acting on long pivoted guide shoes.

The cylinder block is a beautifully detailed aluminum casting with numerous webs and gussets. The cylinder liners are of the wet sleeve type and are aluminum with Nikasil-plated bores. These liners seat on a shoulder forming the bottom of the water jacketing and have a 1 mm flame guard lip at the top to protect the cylinder head gasket.

At the bottom end, iron main bearing caps are cast in place in an aluminum lower crankcase structure (crankshaft saddle). This effectively extends the bearing webs and sides of the crankcase below the crankshaft centerline for maximum structural rigidity and bearing support.

The oil pan is also an aluminum alloy casting incorporating the pickup and baffles. This is supplemented by a fabricated sheet metal windage tray and surge baffles to insure a constant supply of oil with no possibility of cavitation under the

61

highest acceleration forces. From this pickup, oil travels through a passage cast into the block to an eccentric gear oil pump mounted on the crankshaft just forward of the first main bearing. This pump is driven by a flat on the crank and feeds pressure directly through passages in the crankshaft to the main and con rod bearings.

Finally, the forged steel crankshaft bears a family resemblance to that in the familiar L98, but has more elaborate counterweights and a longer nose to accommodate the oil pump drive. The crankshaft is cross-drilled to accommodate internal centrifugal oiling.

Connecting rods are a deep "I" section and are also forged steel. They are joined to the pistons with full floating wrist pins.

The shallow dish forged pistons are of a nearly skirtless "slipper" racing type design. These pistons utilize rings of a special cast iron alloy for compatibility with the Nikasil cylinder bores.

The crankshaft, torsional

Left, an X-ray illustration of the 1989 Corvette ZR1.

Below, a 1989 'Vette with the IMSA GTO add-on kit (James R. Moody photograph).

damper and flywheel are dynamically balanced as a unit before final assembly into the crankcase. All reciprocating parts (rods, pistons, etc.) are balanced in weight and are assembled as matched sets to minimize vibration and stress to produce an extremely smooth running engine and promote longevity.

In sum, the ZR1 represents a quantum increase in sportscar performance. In so doing, it establishes a standard other manufacturers will be hard-pressed to match, much less beat.

Still, although the ZR1 is undoubtedly the greatest Corvette yet, there is certain to be more excitement coming from Chevrolet in the future. The ultimate, final chapter in the story of America's greatest sportscar has not been written. Not by a long shot.

ACKNOWLEDGMENTS

The authors are deeply indebted to a number of individuals without whom this book would not have been possible.

The entire Chevrolet Public Relations staff was unfailingly courteous and helpful. In particular, we would like to thank Ralph Kramer, Ed Lechtzin, Kay Ward, Dave Hederich and Jim Rooney.

We realize it is their job to assist in the publishing of material about Chevrolet cars, but, having worked in this industry for many years, we know that there are people who care and people who are just going through the motions--and, alas, all too many of the latter. The people at Chevy Public Relations really care, and, believe us, it makes a difference.

Ed Lechtzin also supplied additional important material and arranged for our photo shoot of the 1989 'Vettes appearing on pages 58-59, 62-63 and on the back cover. James R. Moody did the shots. Once again, a positive attitude by all counted enormously.

To everyone, our thanks.

As usual, we have tried as hard as we could to ensure the accuracy of the material presented in this book. If we have failed in any regard, please let us know (in care of the address for Bookman Publishing listed in the front of the book) so that future editions may be corrected.

WRITTEN BY THOMAS E. BONSALL AND R. PERRY ZAVITZ

EDITED BY EDWARD A. LEHWALD

GRAPHIC DESIGN BY THOMAS E. BONSALL AND JUDY CRAVEN-MADISON

GRAPHIC PRODUCTION BY HAHN GRAPHICS

PRESS PRODUCTION BY BERTELSMANN PRINTING & MANUFACTURING